2x86 4.2/15

D0535305

Unwrapping the Christmas Crèche

Lisa Flinn and Barbara Younger

Abingdon Press

Nashville

For Claire Eleana Lewis – LNF

For Merple and all the Millers – BKY

Unwrapping the Christmas Crèche

ISBN 0-687-49783-3

Illustrated by Patricia Ludlow

Where's my favorite box? All of these have ornaments.
This is the angel collection. That's the holiday village.
Lights, stockings, tree topper, garlands.
Here it is...

*T*he Christmas crèche.
"Rise and shine," I say in my good-morning voice.
"A whole year has gone by. It's time for you
to tell the story once again.
Places, everyone. It's Advent!"

Good. The stable is right on top.
Stable, you were all the innkeeper could offer to
Mary and Joseph. On that night you welcomed them
with sweet-smelling straw and jingling cowbells.
Now you're the stage for the story.

Behold! It's the Angel. I'm going to be an angel, too
in the play at church. My wings aren't as fancy as yours,
and my robe is stitched from an old sheet.
But I like the part when we all shout, "Good News!"
I'll pretend you are saying it with me. We angels have
a happy role, bringing tidings of great joy.

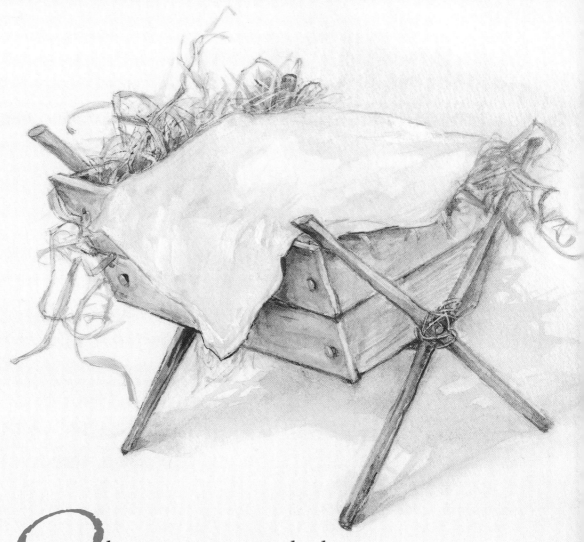

Oh no! Manger, you're broken!
Someone suggests fixing you with glue;
but my dad answers, "We should use carpenter's
tools. No super glue in Bible times."
I rush to get the hammer and tacks.
Maybe the animals wouldn't mind a loose board,
but you're not a crib for fodder anymore. You're a crib
for a real baby, a bed for Baby Jesus.

This must be Him . . . such a tiny bundle.
Here you are, tiny, but the most important figure of
the crèche. Into the manger you go. Sleep, Baby Jesus,
for soon you will wake up the world.

Greetings, Mary, favored one.
I'll put you right next to your baby, so you can take
care of him whenever he needs you.
Mothers are that way.
They like to be near their children.

Joseph? Yes, it's Joseph! For a minute I thought you
were a shepherd. But you have a name:
Joseph, who loved Mary;
Joseph, who led the donkey;
Joseph, who announced the baby's name;
Joseph, whose job wasn't easy.
Joseph, you have a place of honor here.

Baa. You're not one of Bo Peep's sheep or
Mary's little lamb. So what!
It's way better to be a Christmas sheep.

Who's this?
It's you, silly Cow, chewing your cud with half-closed
eyes. Pay attention! Miracles are happening.

Mr. Shepherd with your staff, do you climb out
on ledges to hook missing lambs or use that staff
to hurry along slowpoke sheep?
I wish we were both real shepherds traveling back
in time to that amazing night. We'd startle at the angel's words,
"This will be a sign for you: you will find a child wrapped in
bands of cloth and lying in a manger."
And then we'd cross the fields together searching
for a scene like this one.

I like you, Donkey, with your funny big ears. Sure-footed, you carried Mary from Nazareth to Bethlehem. What a long journey for a mother-to-be. What a great task for a small, gray donkey. Rest now, I'll put you with the others. Rest, Donkey, rest.

Wow! It's the china Beagle that looks exactly like our dog. I found you in the toe of my stocking last year and put you in the crèche. Maybe there really was a dog at the stable. This year, you're a player from the beginning. First you can howl at the camel. Then you can herd the sheep. Next you can make friends with the donkey. But on Christmas Eve, you will guard the baby.

I packed you together last year so you could
trade words of wisdom. One, two, three Wise Men.
You followed the star to the Christ Child.
And you brought presents! God warned you in a
dream to go home by a different road. What did you
think about, talk about, worry about, wonder about,
one, two, three Wise Men?

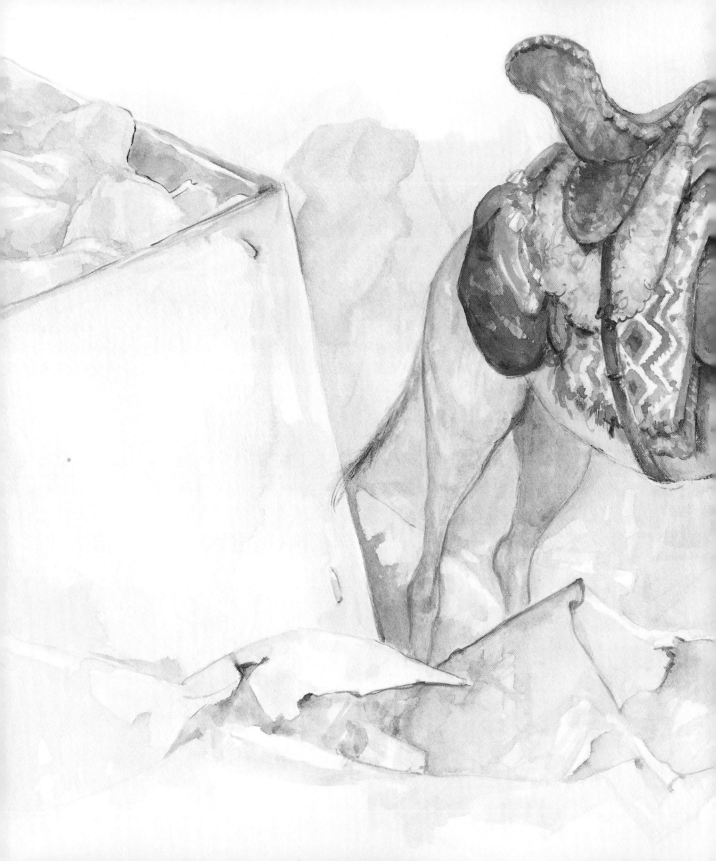

I read about you, Camel, in my social studies book.
They call you the "Ship of the Desert." You can go
days without water across miles and miles of sand.
How far you must have traveled with the Wise Men
from the East. My sister says camels spit.
Don't you dare spit here!

Stars are meant to shine, but the star above the stable
has faded. Star, how can you guide anyone
if you look this dim? I'll tip my brush with glittering
gold paint to brighten you up. Beautiful Star,
you are new again. Shine!

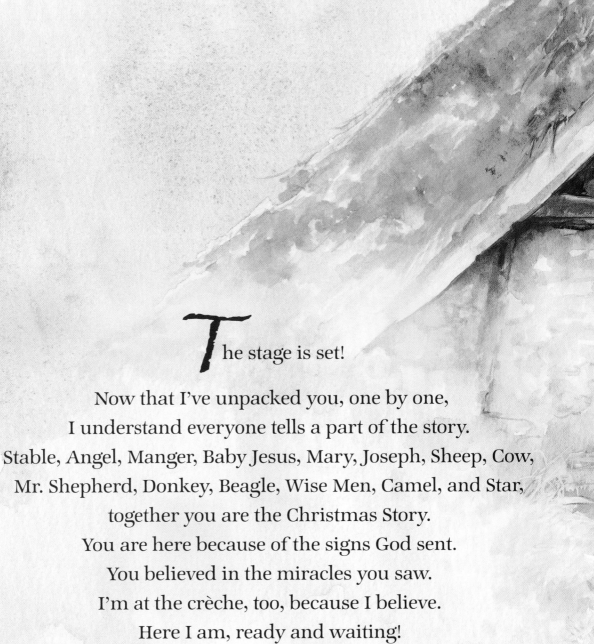

*T*he stage is set!

Now that I've unpacked you, one by one,
I understand everyone tells a part of the story.
Stable, Angel, Manger, Baby Jesus, Mary, Joseph, Sheep, Cow,
Mr. Shepherd, Donkey, Beagle, Wise Men, Camel, and Star,
together you are the Christmas Story.
You are here because of the signs God sent.
You believed in the miracles you saw.
I'm at the crèche, too, because I believe.
Here I am, ready and waiting!

*T*his will be a sign for you:
you will find a child wrapped in
bands of cloth and lying in a manger."
Luke 2:12